The INDIANA BED & BREAKFAST ASSOCIATION COOKBOOK *and* DIRECTORY

Tracy & Phyllis Winters

Winters Publishing
P.O. Box 501
Greensburg, Indiana 47240

(812) 663-4948

PHOTO CREDIT:
Front cover: By Randy O'Rourke

The information about the inns and the recipes were supplied by the inns themselves. The rate information was current at the time of submission, but is subject to change. Every effort has been made to assure that the book is accurate. Neither the inns, authors, or publisher assume responsibility for any errors, whether typographical or otherwise.

Library of Congress Card Catalog Number 91-91443
ISBN 0-9625329-1-6

Dedication

To our daughters,
Rebekah Ann and Rachel Ann
and
To our parents,
Jack and Shirley Winters
and
Wilbur and Marianna Mozingo

With our Love to all of them.

Acknowledgements

We would like to thank The Indiana
Bed & Breakfast Association for working with us
on this project, and all of the innkeepers
who took valuable time to select recipes
and fill out questionnaires. Special thanks to
Karen Lanning for her help.
It is because of all of their efforts that we
were able to make this book a reality.

Preface

Welcome, and have a pleasant journey through the Bed and Breakfasts of Indiana. The recipes presented in this book are just a sampling of what you will encounter in your sojourn through Indiana.

Indiana's Bed and Breakfasts are very diverse. They may be in an historic home or mansion on a quiet street or in a small family home tucked away in the city or on a country road. But they all have one thing in common: the desire to bring a touch of true "Hoosier Hospitality" into your hectic life.

The Indiana Bed and Breakfast Association was formed with specific goals in mind. Topmost we encourage and in fact ask each and every inn to adhere to high standards of cleanliness and safety. Each inn is quality reviewed to assure you of a pleasant stay. Our membership adheres to the highest professional standards.

As you travel throughout Indiana and sample the delicious recipes presented herein you will want to return again and again. For you will have found a home away from home.

Sincerely,

The Indiana Bed and Breakfast Association, Inc.

For more information write:

Indiana Bed and Breakfast Association, Inc.
P.O. Box 1127
Goshen, IN   46526

CONTENTS

MUFFINS

APPLE-CRANBERRY MUFFINS

1 3/4 cups all-purpose flour
1/2 cup sugar
2 1/2 teaspoons baking powder
3/4 teaspoon salt (opt.)
1 egg
3/4 cup milk

1/3 cup oil
1/4 cup rum flavoring (opt.)
1 cup cranberry relish
1 cup finely chopped apple (1)
1 teaspoon cinnamon

In large mixing bowl stir together flour, sugar, baking powder and salt. Make a well in center. Combine egg, milk and oil and add mixture to dry ingredients. Stir till moistened, batter will be lumpy. Add rum flavoring, cranberry relish and apple. Add 1/2 teaspoon of cinnamon. Pour mixture into greased or paper lined cups. Sprinkle remaining cinnamon on muffins. Bake at 400° for 20 - 25 minutes or until golden brown. Serve warm with butter or cream cheese. Yield: 10 - 12 muffins.

Submitted by:

E.B. Rhodes Bed & Breakfast
Rhodes Avenue, P.O. Box 7
West Baden, Indiana 47469
(812) 936-7378
Tom & Tina Hilgediek
$35.00 to $45.00

Full breakfast
4 rooms, 4 private baths
Children allowed, with
  parental supervision
No pets
Restricted smoking
Mastercard & Visa

First edition home was built in 1901. Spacious rooms, decor set in the time period, 2 porches with views. French Lick Railway Museum within walking distance. Patoka Lake with hiking, fishing and other outdoor sports, 15 minutes away.

APPLE-NUT MUFFINS

1 egg
3/4 cup milk
1 medium apple, pared & chopped
1/2 cup vegetable oil
2 cups all-purpose flour

1/3 cup brown sugar
3 teaspoons baking powder
1 teaspoon salt
1/2 teaspoon cinnamon

Topping:
1/4 cup brown sugar

1/4 cup chopped nuts
1/2 teaspoon cinnamon

Heat oven to 400°. Grease muffin pan. Beat egg, stir in milk, apple and oil. Stir in remaining ingredients all at once just until flour is moistened (batter will be lumpy). Fill muffin cups 3/4 full. Sprinkle tops with topping mixture. Bake until golden brown, about 20 minutes. Immediately remove from pan. Yield: 1 dozen muffins.

Submitted by:

The Atwater Century Farm
Bed & Breakfast
4240 W. U.S. 20
LaGrange, Indiana 46761
(219) 463-2743
Martha Lou Neff &
Dianne Hostetler
$50.00 to $75.00

Continental plus breakfast
3 rooms, 1 private bath
Children, over 10
No pets
No smoking

Two story farm house in true country setting. Decorated in country pastels, rooms are filled with family heirlooms. Cozy and quiet, but within driving distance of fine restaurants, craft shops, flea market.

BLUEBERRY MUFFINS

1 3/4 cups sifted all-
 purpose flour
1/4 cup sugar
2 1/2 teaspoons baking
 powder
3/4 teaspoon salt

1 well-beaten egg
3/4 cup milk
1/3 cup cooking oil
1 cup blueberries (fresh
 or frozen)
2 tablespoons sugar

Sift flour, sugar, baking powder, and salt into bowl, make well in center. Combine egg, milk, and oil. Add all at once to dry ingredients. Stir quickly just until dry ingredients are moistened. Toss blueberries (fresh or thawed and well-drained frozen) with 2 tablespoons sugar. Gently stir into batter. Fill greased muffin pans 2/3 full. Bake at 400° about 25 minutes. Yield: 1 dozen muffins.

Submitted by:

Gunn Guest House
904 Park Avenue
Winona Lake, Indiana 46590
(219) 267-7552
Dolores Gunn
$35.00 to $40.00

Full breakfast
4 rooms, 2 shared baths
Children allowed
No pets
No smoking

Victorian home built in 1903 nestled in the heart of historic Winona Lake. Beveled glass windows and some rooms with eight sides. 4 blocks from Grace College and Seminary. Spacious wraparound front porch is across from Rodeheaver Auditorium.

CHERRY BANANA NUT MUFFINS

1 cup sugar
1/2 cup Parkay margarine
(at room temperature)
1 teaspoon vanilla
2 jumbo eggs
2 cups flour
1 teaspoon baking soda

Dash of salt
2 tablespoons cherry
juice
1 jar (10 oz.) maraschino
cherries cut into fourths
3 large bananas mashed)
1 cup walnut halves

Topping:
2 tablespoons brown
sugar
2 tablespoons white
sugar

2 tablespoons finely
chopped walnuts

Mix sugar, Parkay and vanilla until smooth. Add eggs and beat 1 - 2 minutes. Blend flour, soda and salt, and stir into egg mixture. Add cherry juice. Stir only to blend. Add cherries, bananas and nuts. Stir to blend. Put in 12 muffin cups. Blend topping ingredients. Top muffins with topping. Bake at 350° for 25 minutes. Yield: 12 muffins.

Submitted by:

Cragwood Inn
303 N. Second
Decatur, Indiana 46733
(219) 728-2000
George & Nancy Craig
$45.00 to $75.00

Continental plus breakfast
4 rooms, 2 private baths
Children, over 10
No pets
Restricted smoking
Mastercard & Visa

Queen Anne house with magnificent woodwork and beveled leaded glass. Innovative weekends include Victorian crafts, fine needlework seminars, mystery parties, chocolate lovers' weekend and herbal crafting.

KIWI GUAVA MUFFINS

1 1/2 cups all-purpose flour
1 1/2 teaspoons baking soda
1 1/2 teaspoons baking powder
1/4 teaspoon salt
1/2 cup margarine or butter, softened
3/4 cup sugar
1 teaspoon vanilla extract
2 eggs
1/2 cup canned guava nectar
1 cup kiwi fruit, peeled & diced (2)

Preheat oven to 400°. Combine flour, baking soda, baking powder, and salt; reserve. Cream butter, sugar, and vanilla until light and fluffy. Beat in eggs, one at a time, on low speed. Beat in half the flour mixture and then the guava nectar. Add remaining flour mixture; mix just until blended. Fold in kiwi fruit. Divide batter among muffin cups filling almost to the top. Bake 18 - 20 minutes or until toothpick inserted in center comes out clean. Cool muffins on a wire rack. Yield: About 12 muffins.

Submitted by:

Gray Goose Inn
350 Indian Boundary Road
Chesterton, Indiana 46304
(219) 926-5781
Tim Wilk & Chuck Ramsey
$72.00 to $85.00

Full breakfast
5 rooms, 5 private baths
Children, over 12
No pets
Restricted smoking
Mastercard, Visa, Am Ex, Discover

Located in Chesterton, Gateway to the Indiana Dunes State & National Lakeshore. Surrounded by 100 wooded acres, overlooking Lake Palomara. Trails, boats, bikes, fireplaces, in-room phones. Near I-80 - 90 and I-94. 1 hour from Chicago, 2 1/2 hours from Indianapolis.

LEMON PECAN MUFFINS

1 3/4 cups sifted all-purpose flour
1/2 cup + 3 tablespoons sugar
3 teaspoons baking powder
1 teaspoon salt
2/3 cup chopped pecans

1 egg
1/2 cup milk
1/2 teaspoon grated lemon peel
2 tablespoons lemon juice
1/3 cup oil

Lemon Sugar Topping:
1 1/2 tablespoons flour
1/4 cup sugar

1 teaspoon grated lemon peel
1 tablespoon margarine
Pecan halves

Sift flour, sugar, baking powder and salt; add pecans. Beat egg lightly, add milk, lemon peel, lemon juice and oil. Add to flour mixture, stir just until all dry ingredients are moistened. Spoon into greased muffin cups. Combine ingredients for Lemon Sugar Topping (cut together with pastry blender) until crumbly. Top muffins with Topping and a pecan half. Bake in preheated 400° oven for about 20 minutes or until lightly browned and baked through. Remove carefully from muffin tin after 1 or 2 minutes. Serve warm or cold. Makes 12 muffins.

Submitted by:

Purviance House
326 South Jefferson
Huntington, Indiana 46750
(219) 356-4218
Bob & Jean Gernand
$35.00 to $50.00

Full breakfast
3 rooms, 2 private baths
Children allowed
No pets
Restricted smoking
Discover

Elegant 1859 Greek Revival-Italianate on National Register of Historic Places. Winding cherry staircase, ornate ceiling designs, unique parquet floors and 4 unusually designed fireplaces. Lovingly restored and decorated with period furnishings to create a warm, inviting atmosphere.

MAPLE WALNUT (OR PECAN) MUFFINS

1 1/2 cups chopped walnuts or pecans
3 tablespoons unsalted butter, softened
2 eggs
1 cup whipping cream
1 1/4 cups pure maple syrup (no substitute)
1 teaspoon maple or vanilla extract
1 1/2 cups flour
1 1/2 cups old-fashioned rolled oats
1 tablespoon ground cinnamon
2 teaspoons baking powder
1 teaspoon baking soda
1 cup chopped dates

Preheat oven to 350°. Line 18 muffin cups with paper liners. Grease spaces between cups or muffin tins so side of muffin doesn't stick to the pan. Mix nuts and butter together on a baking sheet and toast in oven for 5 minutes, stirring a time or two. Remove from oven. Beat eggs, cream, 1 cup maple syrup and extract together in mixing bowl. Combine flour, oats, cinnamon, baking powder, and baking soda. Stir into egg mixture just until combined. Stir in dates and 1 cup of toasted nuts. Fill muffin cups 3/4 full with batter. Sprinkle tops with the rest of toasted nuts and drizzle each muffin with part of the remaining 1/4 cup maple syrup. Bake for 20 minutes or until it tests done. Makes 18 muffins.

Submitted by:

The Apple Inn
604 South Brady
Attica, Indiana 47918
(317) 762-6574
Carolyn Carlson & Don Martin
$40.00 to $60.00

Continental plus breakfast
5 rooms, 1 private bath
Children, over 12
No pets
Restricted smoking

Step back into time in this 1903 Colonial Revival home (Brady St. Historic District). Guests greeted with Victorian charm: spiced apple cider, homemade pie or an old-fashioned banana split. Unique theme bedrooms.

MOTHER DEWITT'S MUFFINS

1 cup rolled oats
1/2 cup brown sugar
1 cup buttermilk
1/2 cup oil
1 cup flour
1 teaspoon baking
   powder

3 teaspoons vanilla
1 teaspoon nutmeg
1 teaspoon cinnamon
8 oz. box chopped dates

Soak first three ingredients for 10 minutes. Mix ingredients in order.
Preheat oven to 400°. Bake for 15 - 20 minutes. Yield: 12 muffins.
(Note: Makes great mini-muffins, bake for 10 - 12 minutes.)

Submitted by:

The Candlelight Inn
503 E. Fort Wayne Street
Warsaw, Indiana 46580
(219) 267-2906
William & Deborah Hambright
$58.00 to $76.00

Full breakfast
4 rooms, 4 private baths
Children, over 10
No pets
No smoking
Mastercard, Visa, Am Ex

Victorian decor of restored 1860's home is reminiscent of "Gone With
the Wind". Elegant parlor, antiques, and candlelight. Near many
points of local interest. You'll feel welcome and want to return often
to our romantic atmosphere.

PEACHY MUFFINS

1 cup wheat bran cereal
1 cup orange or apple
  juice
1 teaspoon baking soda
1 cup nonfat buttermilk
1 cup quick oats
  (uncooked)
1 cup dried peaches
  (chopped)

1 cup raisins
1/2 cup whole wheat
flour
1/2 cup all-purpose flour
1/3 cup Sweet 'n Low
  (4 packets)
1/2 teaspoon salt (opt.)
Vegetable spray

Combine cereal and juice in bowl. Dissolve baking soda in buttermilk, mix. Add buttermilk, oats and remaining ingredients to cereal and stir until well moistened. Coat muffin pans with cooking spray, filling 2/3 full. Preheat oven to 375° and bake for 20 minutes. Yield: 18 - 20 muffins, approximately 120 calories each.

Submitted by:

Publick House
28 Duck Creek Crossing
P.O. Box 202
Metamora, Indiana 47030
(317) 647-6729 or
(513) 941-2588
Pat Breuer & Natalie Becker
$50.00 to $70.00

Full breakfast
4 rooms, 3 private baths
Children, over 10
No pets
Restricted smoking
Mastercard & Visa

Circa 1850 frontier architecture in an historic arts & crafts canal town featuring horse drawn canal boat rides, operating aqueduct and grist mill. Delicious gourmet meals served in coziness of your room. Over 120 shops. Walk to all shops. Cable T.V.

PUMPKIN APPLE STREUSEL MUFFINS

2 1/2 cups all-purpose
  flour
2 cups sugar
1 tablespoon pumpkin
  pie spice
1 teaspoon baking soda
1/2 teaspoon salt (opt.)

2 eggs, lightly beaten
1 cup Libby's solid pack
  pumpkin
1/2 cup vegetable oil
2 cups peeled finely
  chopped apples

Streusel topping:
2 tablespoons flour
1/4 cup sugar

1/2 teaspoon ground
  cinnamon
4 teaspoons butter

Preheat oven to 350°. In large bowl combine first 5 ingredients, set aside. In medium bowl, combine eggs, pumpkin and oil. Add liquid ingredients to dry ingredients. Stir just until moistened. Stir in apples. Spoon batter into greased or paper lined muffin cups. Fill 3/4 full. For Streusel topping: In small bowl combine flour, sugar and cinnamon. Cut in butter until mixture is crumbly. Sprinkle topping over muffin batter. Bake for 35 - 40 minutes or until toothpick comes out clean. Yield: 18 muffins. Variation: For 6 giant muffins, increase baking time to 40 - 45 minutes.

Submitted by:

Market Street Bed & Breakfast
253 E. Market Street
Nappanee, Indiana 46550
(219) 773-2261
Jean Janc
$40.00 to $55.00

Full breakfast
6 rooms, 4 private baths
Children, over 12
No pets
Restricted smoking
Mastercard & Visa

We are in the town where Amish Acres is located. We serve a delicious full breakfast, and are near Colonial Williamsburg. Also we are 40 minutes from Notre Dame.

RAISIN BRAN MUFFINS

1 1/2 cups All-Bran cereal	1/4 cup vegetable oil
1 1/4 cups milk	1 cup raisins
1 egg	1 1/4 cups flour
1/2 cup brown sugar	1 tablespoon baking powder
1/4 teaspoon salt	

In large mixing bowl combine All-Bran cereal and milk. Let stand 3 minutes or until cereal softens. Add eggs, sugar, salt, and oil and mix well. Add raisins. Add flour and baking powder, stir only until combined. Grease muffin pan. Bake at 400° for 20 minutes. Yield: 12 muffins.

Submitted by:

Bauer House
4595 N. Maple Grove Road
Bloomington, Indiana 47404
(812) 336-4383
Frank & Beverly Bauer
$40.00

Continental plus breakfast
3 rooms, 1 private bath
Children allowed
No pets
Restricted smoking

Historic red brick farmhouse built in 1865. Nestled in the rolling hills of Southern Indiana. Surrounded by dry stone walls with a spacious front yard. Plenty of space for roaming the area by bike or on foot. 3 miles from the heart of downtown Bloomington and Indiana University.

RHUBARB MUFFINS

1 1/4 cups brown sugar
1 egg
1/2 cup oil
2 teaspoons vanilla
  extract
1 cup buttermilk
1 1/2 cups diced rhubarb
  (can use frozen)
Topping:
1 tablespoon butter,
  softened
1/3 cup sugar

2 1/2 cups all-purpose
  flour
1 teaspoon baking soda
1 teaspoon baking
  powder
1/2 teaspoon salt

2 teaspoons cinnamon
1/3 cup slivered almonds

Combine brown sugar, egg, oil, vanilla and buttermilk in a bowl. Add rhubarb. In a separate bowl, stir together flour, soda, baking powder and salt. Add dry ingredients to the other ingredients. Stir until just blended. Use muffin papers and fill each 2/3 full. Sprinkle with topping mixture. Bake at 400° for 20 - 25 minutes. Yield: 1 1/2 dozen muffins.

Submitted by:

The Hoffman House
P.O. Box 906
Indianapolis, Indiana 46206
(317) 635-1701 (eff. 10/1/91)
Laura A. Arnold
$40.00 to $75.00

Continental plus breakfast
2 rooms
Children, over 12
No pets
Restricted smoking
Mastercard & Visa

American four-square house built in 1903 and 1.5 miles from Monument Circle. Both guest rooms feature double beds adorned with handmade quilts. Special services for business travelers: photocopier, FAX and IBM compatible computer with modem.

SPECIAL BLUEBERRY MUFFINS

1/2 cup rolled oats	1/2 teaspoon salt
1/2 cup orange juice	1/4 teaspoon baking
1 1/2 cups flour	soda
1/2 cup sugar	1/2 cup oil
1 1/4 teaspoons baking	1 egg
powder	1 cup+ thawed, frozen
	or fresh blueberries

Topping:

1/4 teaspoon cinnamon	2 tablespoons sugar

Preheat oven to 400°. In large bowl combine oats and orange juice. Stir well. Add flour, sugar, baking powder, salt, soda, oil and egg. Mix well. Stir in berries. Spoon into prepared muffin tins, fill 2/3 full. Sprinkle with topping mixture. Bake 18 - 20 minutes until golden brown. Serve warm. Yield: 12 muffins.

Submitted by:

Hans Haus of Berne
166 Columbia Street
Berne, Indiana 46711
(219) 589-3793
John & Ginger Hans
$25.00 per room

Full or Continental plus
breakfast
3 rooms, 1 private bath
Children allowed
No pets
No smoking

Built in 1905, this Victorian style home is located in the heart of the largest Swiss & Amish settlement in the Midwest. The wraparound porch takes you to a private entrance upstairs to the nicely decorated, spacious guest rooms.

SQUASH MUFFINS

2 cups cooked, mashed winter squash
1 1/2 cups light brown sugar, packed
1/2 cup molasses
1 cup soft butter

2 eggs, beaten
3 1/2 cups flour
2 teaspoons baking soda
1/2 teaspoon salt
1/2 cup chopped pecans

Cook, drain, and mash squash to the consistency of mashed potatoes. Cream sugar, molasses and butter. Add eggs and squash and blend well. Mix flour with soda and salt. Blend into the squash batter. Fold in nuts. Fill paper-lined or greased muffin tin about 1/2 full. Bake at 375° for 20 minutes or until they test done. After muffins are cool, wrap well and freeze any leftovers. Makes 2 dozen or more muffins. This is an Amish recipe.

Submitted by:

Tyler's Place
19562 St. Rd. 120 West
Bristol, Indiana 46507
(219) 848-7145
Ron & Esther Tyler
$40.00 to $45.00

Full breakfast
2 rooms
Children allowed
No pets
Restricted smoking

Original home of Raber Golf Course greens keeper, with beautiful view of the 27 hole golf course. Common room is decorated with an Amish flavor. Breakfast served in Florida room during warm weather. Evenings enjoyed in the backyard around a fire ring.

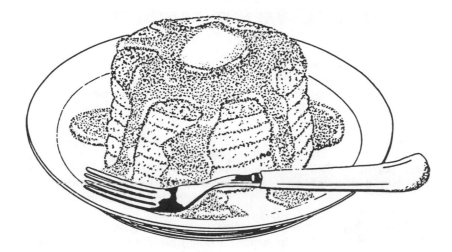

PANCAKES
&
FRENCH TOAST

BANANA WALNUT PANCAKES

1 cup unbleached flour	2 cups buttermilk, room
1 cup whole wheat flour	temperature
1/4 cup wheat germ	6 tablespoons honey
1 tablespoon baking	2 ripe medium bananas,
powder	peeled & mashed
1 1/2 teaspoons baking	1/2 cup finely chopped
soda	walnuts
Salt (opt.)	Maple syrup
1/4 cup safflower oil	Vanilla yogurt, cinnamon
	& additional bananas

In large bowl, stir together flours, wheat germ, baking powder, baking soda and salt to taste. In separate bowl, beat eggs. Mix in oil, buttermilk, honey and bananas, mixing well. Stir in nuts. Pour egg mixture into dry ingredients. Stir just until dry ingredients are moistened. Brush hot griddle or skillet lightly with additional oil. Drop 1/4 cup batter per pancake onto griddle and spread with spoon to make a flat pancake. Cook over medium heat until lightly browned on bottom and bubbles form on top. Pancakes burn easily. Turn and brown lightly on second side, 1 - 2 minutes. Serve with maple syrup or vanilla yogurt flavored with cinnamon and sliced bananas. Makes about 20 pancakes.

Submitted by:

Story Inn	Full breakfast
P.O. Box 64	13 rooms, 12 private baths
Nashville, Indiana 47448	Children allowed
(812) 988-2273	Pets allowed
Benjamin & Cynthia Schultz	Restricted smoking
$65.00 to $125.00	Mastercard, Visa, Am Ex,
	Discover

Located on southern edge of Brown County State Park, we have a Dodge City-designed general store housing a critically acclaimed full-service restaurant. Overnight lodging upstairs and in the surrounding cottages. Rooms furnished with period antiques and original art work. Air-conditioned.

BEECHWOOD LEMON CREPES

Favorite pancake batter
  (use pkg. measurement)
1 cup milk

Powdered sugar
1 teaspoon lemon juice
  (for each crepe)

Using your favorite pancake batter, add 1 cup of milk to recipe, or a little more if batter seems too thick. On grill or in Teflon skillet, fry pancakes between 8 - 10 inches in diameter. Remove and keep warm. To serve, spread each with a light layer of powdered sugar. Add a teaspoon or so of fresh lemon juice in a horizontal line down each crepe. Roll crepes in a line with lemon juice. Serve 3 on each plate and sprinkle with powdered sugar. Serve with bacon or sausage.

Submitted by:

Beechwood Inn
Frontage Road
Batesville, Indiana 47006
(812) 934-3426
Posey Romweber
$60.00 to $85.00

Continental plus breakfast
4 rooms, 4 private baths
Children allowed
No pets
Smoking allowed
Mastercard & Visa

Beautiful red brick traditional home on 5 acres with a forest behind. Warm, roomy, private phones, televisions in all rooms. Lots of golf courses nearby. Also Nashville and Metamora for the craft lovers.

CRUNCHY OVEN FRENCH TOAST

3 eggs
1 cup half-and-half
1 teaspoon vanilla
2 tablespoons sugar
1/4 teaspoon salt

3 cups Corn Flakes,
  crushed to 1 cup
8 diagonally-cut slices of
  French bread - 3/4"
  thick

Grease 15" x 10" x 1" baking dish. In shallow bowl combine liquid ingredients. Add sugar and salt. Dip bread in egg mixture: eggs, half-and-half, vanilla, sugar, and salt. Cover bread well, then dip in Corn Flake crumbs. Place in greased pan, freeze 1 to 2 hours. Heat oven to 425°, bake 15 - 20 minutes until golden brown, turning once. Serve with strawberry or blueberry syrup. Garnish with fresh fruit.

Submitted by:

Timberidge Bed & Breakfast
16801 St. Rd. 4
Goshen, Indiana 46526
(219) 533-7133
Donita M. Brookmyer
$50.00 to $70.00

Continental plus breakfast
1 suite, 1 private bath
Children, over 3
No pets
No smoking

Guests enjoy privacy of a master suite with Victorian furnished bedroom, sitting room with sofa sleeper, private entrance, television, air-conditioning, wood burning stove. The best of city & country - close to town, yet removed to the majestic beauty of the woods for nature-lovers. We welcome those of you with an affinity for the country.

LOOKOUT'S APPLE PANCAKES

1 cup chopped apple (1 good-sized apple)	3/4 teaspoon salt
2 tablespoons sugar	1/8 teaspoon cinnamon
1 1/4 cups unbleached flour	2 tablespoons sugar
1/4 cup wheat germ	1 egg, well beaten
3 1/2 teaspoons baking powder	1 cup milk
	3 tablespoons vegetable oil

Sprinkle the chopped apple with 2 tablespoons sugar and set aside. Stir together flour, wheat germ, baking powder, salt, cinnamon and sugar. Add milk and oil to egg and stir liquids into dry mixture. Stir just until moistened. Add sweetened apple. Bake on hot griddle (350°). Serve with honey or syrup, and sausages. Makes 8 - 10 pancakes.

Submitted by:

The Lookout Bed & Breakfast	Full breakfast
14544 C. R. 12	5 rooms, 3 private baths
Middlebury, Indiana 46540	Children allowed
(219) 825-9809	No pets
Mary-Lou & Jim Wolfe	Restricted smoking
$45.00 to $70.00	

Hilltop country home in Northeastern Indiana Amish country, furnished with antiques & collectibles. Near Shipshewana Auction and Flea Market, lots of antique, craft and gift shops, great restaurants, & 1832 Bonneyville Mill. Enjoy great hospitality, spectacular view, private swimming pool, wooded trails and wildflower garden.

ORANGE-ALMOND FRENCH TOAST

1/4 cup butter
1/3 cup sugar
1/4 teaspoon cinnamon
1 - 2 teaspoons grated
   orange zest
1/3 cup sliced almonds

4 eggs, slightly beaten
2/3 cup orange juice
8 thick slices French or
   Italian bread
   (homemade if possible)

Preheat oven to 325°. Melt butter in jelly roll pan or other pan which will hold bread and contain the butter. Sprinkle sugar, cinnamon, orange zest and almonds evenly over butter. Combine eggs and juice. Dip bread into egg mixture, place in pan on butter mixture. Bake 20 minutes. Serve nut side up with raspberry or cinnamon syrup. Makes 4 servings. This recipe is great for B&B cooks who sometimes need 5 hands to get breakfast done all at one time. It can bake while you're doing something else.

Submitted by:

The Nuthatch B&B
7161 Edgewater Place
Indianapolis, Indiana 46240
(317) 257-2660
Joan H. Morris
$65.00 to $125.00 *
 * Except Indy 500 weekend

Full breakfast
2 rooms, 2 private baths
Children, over 12
No pets
Restricted smoking
Am Ex

1920's French country cottage with arched windows and leaded glass doors, overlooking White River as it wends its way south past Broad Ripple Village. In a resort-like setting minutes north of downtown Indianapolis. Breakfasts are special from exotic to "Hoosier-home-cookin'," and all from scratch.

OVEN-BAKED FRENCH BREAD

1 loaf French or Italian bread, sliced 1" thick 3 eggs 2/3 cup milk	2 teaspoons vanilla 3 tablespoons sugar Cinnamon to taste

Mix batter ingredients and dip bread slices until covered well. Melt 1/2 stick margarine in cookie sheet or 9" x 13" pan. Fit slices into pan, bake at 400° for 15 minutes, then turn slices over. Watch closely. Serve with fresh blueberries, with sour cream and spoonful of brown sugar on top. Makes 4 servings.

Submitted by:

Coneygar B&B 54835 Co. Rd. 33 Middlebury, Indiana 46540 (219) 825-5707 Mary Dugdale Hankins $30.00 to $70.00	Full breakfast 3 rooms, 1 private bath Children allowed Pets allowed Restricted smoking

Country home on 40 acres, with fireplaces, primitive antiques, original art. Screened-in porch. Northern Indiana Amish country nearby: shops, restaurants, Shipshewana flea market, overnight horse stabling, wheelchair designed home, near many historic attractions.

OVERNIGHT FRENCH TOAST

1 long, thin loaf French
 bread
6 large eggs
2 1/2 cups milk
1 tablespoon sugar

1/4 teaspoon salt
2 teaspoons vanilla
1 1/2 tablespoons
 butter, cut into pieces

Butter a 2-quart or 9" x 11" dish.   Slice bread into 1" thick slices.
Arrange bread in one layer in buttered dish. Beat together eggs,
milk, sugar, salt and vanilla. Pour over bread. Cover and refrigerate 4
to 36 hours. Dot top with butter and bake at 350° for 45 to 50
minutes or until puffy. Serve with warm syrup.

Submitted by:

1887 Black Dog Inn
2830 Untalulti
Monticello, Indiana 47960
(219) 583-8297
Joyce, Tom,, & 'Bo' Condo
$59.00 to $89.00

Continental plus breakfast
5 rooms, 5 private baths
Children allowed
Pets allowed
Restricted smoking
Mastercard & Visa

Peace and charm await you at our Indiana farm style home. Beautiful
grounds, wickered summer porch, queen four-postered beds, our
lake, boating, swimming, fishing, amusement park, antiques, and
auctions all near at hand. Come and enjoy an American classic!

BAKED GOODS

Rolls, Cookies, Cakes & Breads

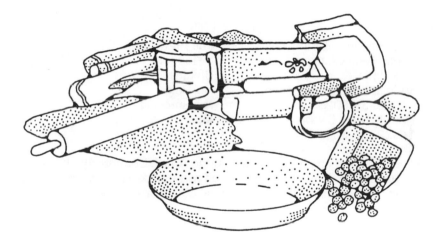

AMISH CHURCH COOKIES

5 cups sugar
2 1/2 cups lard
1 cup molasses
1 cup hot water
4 eggs
2 teaspoons vanilla

2 teaspoons ginger
1/2 teaspoon cinnamon
1 teaspoon baking
  powder
12-15 cups flour

Dissolve 3 tablespoons soda and 1 teaspoon salt in hot water. Set aside. Cream sugar and lard together. Add molasses, hot water mixture and eggs. Beat well. Add rest of ingredients in order listed. Mix well. Roll out and cut in your favorite shape. Bake at 375° for 10 - 15 minutes.

Submitted by:

Bee Hive Bed & Breakfast
  and Guest Cottage
Box 1191
Middlebury, Indiana 46540
(219)825 - 5023
Herb & Treva Swarm
$49.,95 to $60.00

Full Breakfast
3 Rooms
Children Allowed
No Pets
No Smoking
MasterCard, Visa

The Bee Hive is on a farm, located in the Amish Community. It is built with hand sawn lumber, with exposed red oak beams. A loft crowns the sitting and kitchen area. Many local attractions in the area.

BISCUITS

2 1/4 cups flour
4 teaspoons baking powder
1/2 teaspoon salt
1/2 teaspoon cream of tartar

2 tablespoons sugar
6 tablespoons golden Crisco shortening
2/3 cup milk
1 egg

Combine dry ingredients with shortening. Combine egg and milk, add to shortening mixture, mix with a fork. Turn onto lightly floured board and knead 5-6 times. Pat or roll lightly to 1/2" thickness. Cut and bake on ungreased cookie sheet at 425° for 10-12 minutes. Makes 12-14 biscuits.

Submitted by:

Weavers Country Oaks
0310 N. U.S. 20
LaGrange, Indiana 46761 or
P.O. Box 632
Shipshewana, Indiana 46565
(219) 768-7191 or
1-800-426-2029
Catherine & LaMar Weaver
$50.00 to $65.00 & tax

Full breakfast
4 bedrooms, 1 private bath
Children allowed
No pets
Restricted smoking

On 3 1/2 acres of lovely oak trees, overlooking Amish countryside, 4 miles from downtown Shipshewana. Majestic landscaping, weekend getaways or small retreats encouraged. Upper level of home has 3 bedrooms, kitchen, dining room, and common room and shared bath. Lower level has 1 room with private bath.

BREAKFAST OATMEAL COOKIES

1 cup butter or margarine	1 teaspoon baking powder
1 cup brown sugar	1 teaspoon salt
1 cup white sugar	3 cups oatmeal (regular or quick)
2 eggs	1 cup raisins
1 teaspoon vanilla	1 cup pecans or walnuts
1 1/2 cups flour	
1 teaspoon baking soda	

Cream butter and sugars. Add eggs and vanilla. Sift dry ingredients (flour, soda, baking powder and salt), add to butter mixture. Add oatmeal, raisins and nuts. Drop by teaspoonfuls onto cookie sheet. Bake at 350° for 10 minutes. Makes 40 cookies. Recipe can be doubled, using half butter, half margarine. BEST OATMEAL COOKIES EVER!

Submitted by:

The Book Inn
508 W. Washington
South Bend, Indiana 46601
(219) 288-1990
Peggy & John Livingston
$75.00

Continental plus breakfast
5 rooms, 5 private baths
Children, over 16
No pets
No smoking
Mastercard, Visa, Am Ex

120 year old Second Empire home in beautiful downtown South Bend. A 1991 Decorator's Showcase home with every space elegantly designed. Breakfasts served with fine china, silver, candlelight and fresh flowers.

CHOPPED APPLE CAKE

2 cups diced apples
3 eggs
1 3/4 cups sugar
1 cup oil
1 cup nuts

2 cups flour
1 teaspoon salt
1 teaspoon baking soda
1 teaspoon cinnamon

Glaze:
1/2 cup brown sugar
1/2 cup white sugar
2 tablespoons flour

1 cup water
1/2 stick margarine
1 teaspoon vanilla

Mix first five ingredients, then add the remainder of cake ingredients. Bake at 350° for 1 hour in greased bundt pan. Boil glaze ingredients until thick, poke holes in cake, pour glaze onto cake.

Submitted by:

The Cliff House B&B
122 Fairmount Drive
Madison, Indiana 47250
(812) 265-5272
Jae Breitweiser
$55.00 to $82.50

Continental plus breakfast
6 rooms, 6 private baths
Children allowed
No pets
Restricted smoking
Mastercard & Visa

Located high on a bluff overlooking historic downtown Madison & Ohio River. Candlelit breakfast served on Haviland china 8-10 A.M. Evening snack plates of homemade chocolate chip cookies, fresh fruit and mints provided for guests.

CINNAMON CHEESE COFFEE CAKE

1 tube of crescent rolls	1/2 cup sugar
8 ozs. cream cheese	1 egg yolk
1/2 teaspoon vanilla	
Topping:	1/2 teaspoon cinnamon
1/4 cup sugar	1/4 cup chopped nuts

Lay half of crescent rolls flat in 8" x 8" pan. Soften cream cheese. Mix vanilla, sugar and egg yolk into cream cheese. Spoon this mixture over dough. Lay remaining half of crescent rolls on top. Mix topping ingredients and sprinkle over dough. Bake at 350° for 30 - 35 minutes. Makes 8 slices.

Submitted by:

Boone Docks on the River
7159 Edgewater Place
Indianapolis, Indiana 46240
(317) 257-3671
Lynne & Mike Boone
$50.00 to $60.00

Full breakfast
1 room, 1 private bath
Children allowed
No pets
Restricted smoking

A 1920's English Tudor cottage located along White River in a casual resort-like setting. Enjoy the quiet English charm of the River Room suite and relax on the main deck or the riverside deck.

CINNAMON ROLLS

1 cup all-purpose flour
3 tablespoons sugar
2 pkgs. dry yeast
  (rapid rise)
1 1/2 teaspoons salt
2/3 cup powdered milk

2 1/2 tablespoons butter
  or margarine (melted)
1 1/2 cups hot water
  from tap
2 1/2 cups all-purpose
  flour

Filling:
1/4 cup melted butter
1 cup brown sugar,
  firmly packed

1 tablespoon cinnamon
1 teaspoon nutmeg

Mix 1 cup flour, sugar, yeast, salt and powdered milk well, add liquids and mix well again. Add 2 1/2 cups flour and mix well. Place in oiled bowl and let rise to double in size, about 2 1/2 hours. Punch down. Place on floured surface, knead 10 - 12 times. Roll into rectangle. Brush with melted butter. Mix other filling ingredients and sprinkle over butter. Roll like a jelly roll, slice in 1" slices and place in buttered 9" x 13" pan. Let rise to double in size. Bake at 350° for 20 minutes. Yield: 20 rolls.

Submitted by:

Morgan's Farm Country
Bed & Breakfast
RR #2
Austin, Indiana 47102
(812) 794-2536
Norma Bebout &
Brenda Stamper
$55.00 to $80.00

Full breakfast
4 rooms, 4 private baths
Children allowed
Stables/Kennels available
Restricted smoking
Mastercard & Visa

A unique Bed & Breakfast featuring Williamsburg style home set on 100 acres of rolling countryside. Walk in the woods or swim in the pool. Animals on the estate include buffalo, peacocks, swans and horses. Near cities and historic attractions with easy access to I-65.

FRUIT SWIRL COFFEE CAKE

1 1/2 cups sugar
1 cup margarine
1 1/2 teaspoon baking
powder
1 teaspoon vanilla

1 teaspoon almond
extract
4 eggs
3 cups all-purpose flour
1 - 21 oz. can cherry,
apricot, or blueberry
pie filling

Glaze:
1 cup powdered sugar

1 - 2 tablespoons milk

Heat oven to 350°. Grease jellyroll pan (15 1/2" x 10 1/2" x 1"). Beat sugar, margarine, baking powder, vanilla, almond extract, and eggs in large bowl until blended. Beat on high speed for 3 minutes. Stir in flour. Spread 2/3 of batter in pan. Spread pie filling over batter. Drop remaining batter by teaspoonfuls onto pie filling. Bake until light brown, about 45 minutes. Beat powdered sugar and milk for glaze until smooth. Drizzle with glaze while warm.

Submitted by:

Yoder's Zimmer mit Fr>üstück
  Haus
P.O. Box 1396
504 S. Main
Middlebury, Indiana 46540
(219) 825-2378
Wilbur & Evelyn Yoder
$40.00 to $50.00

Full breakfast
5 rooms
Children allowed
No pets
No smoking
Mastercard & Visa

In the heart of northern Indiana's Amish Country near Shipshewana flea market and auction, and craft, gift & antique shops. We delight in sharing our Amish-Mennonite heritage with guests. Modern air-conditioned home decorated with family heirlooms and collectibles.

NETTIE'S BANANA BREAD (OR MUFFINS)

1/2 cup Crisco shortening	2 cups flour
1 cup sugar	1/4 teaspoon salt
2 eggs	3 medium bananas, mashed
3 tablespoons milk	1/2 cup chopped nuts
1 teaspoon baking soda	

Cream shortening, gradually add sugar. Add eggs and beat until light and fluffy. Dissolve soda in milk. Add salt to flour. Add milk and flour alternately to shortening mixture. Stir in bananas and nuts. Pour into greased and floured loaf pan. Bake in preheated 350° oven for 45 minutes or until toothpick inserted comes out clean. Makes 1 loaf. Bread can be wrapped and sealed tightly and frozen for 2 months.

Submitted by:

Braxtan House Inn B&B	Full breakfast
210 N. Gospel St.	6 rooms, 6 private baths
Paoli, Indiana 47454	Children, over 12
(812) 723-4877	No pets
Terry & Brenda Cornwell	Restricted smoking
$45.00 to $70.00	Mastercard, Visa, Discover

1893 Queen Anne Victorian, with 21 rooms, six of which are guest rooms. Furnished in antiques, large veranda with wicker furniture. Antique shop on premises. On National Register, with ski resort 2 miles away, and 2 state parks twenty minutes away. In Southern Indiana's beautiful hills.

PECAN ROLLS

1 pkg. Rich's frozen roll dough	2/3 cup sugar
1 pkg. regular butterscotch pudding	1 teaspoon cinnamon
	1 cup pecans
	1 stick margarine, melted

Mix pudding with sugar and cinnamon. Spray bundt pan with Pam. Arrange frozen rolls in pan. Cover with pecans. Sprinkle pudding mixture over rolls. Pour melted butter over all. Let rise overnight. Bake in preheated 350° oven for 25 minutes. Makes 24 rolls.

Submitted by:

The River Belle	Continental plus breakfast
P.O. Box 669	6 rooms, 2 private baths
Grandview, Indiana 47635	Children allowed
(812) 649-2500	No pets
Don & Pat Phillips	No smoking
$45.00 to $65.00	Mastercard & Visa

1866 mansion resembles old river showboat with wraparound gingerbread porches. Four-poster beds, lacy curtains, heirloom antiques, oriental rugs and river views. Private cottage. Area attractions include River Park & Lincoln State Park, & Holiday World.

PERSIMMON BREAD

2/3 cup shortening	1/2 teaspoons baking
2 2/3 cup sugar	powder
4 eggs	1 teaspoon cinnamon
2 cups persimmon pulp	1 teaspoon cloves
2/3 cup water	2/3 cup nuts
3 1/3 cups flour	2/3 cup raisins
2 teaspoons baking soda	

Cream shortening and sugar until fluffy. Stir in eggs, pulp, and water. Blend flour, soda, baking powder and spices. Stir in nuts and raisins. Bake in loaf pans with waxed paper on the bottom. Bake at 350° for 60-70 minutes. Makes 3 loaves. Note: 1 gallon of persimmons equals 4 cups of pulp.

Submitted by:

Lanning House Bed &
  Breakfast & 1920 Annex
206 E. Poplar St.
Salem, Indiana 47167
(812) 883-3484
Mrs. Jeanette Hart
$30.00 to $50.00

Full breakfast
7 rooms, 4 private baths
Children allowed
No pets
No smoking
Personal checks accepted

House is part of the Salem Museum, built by Azariah Lanning after returning from the Civil War. Louisville Kentucky Derby just 45 minutes away. Near Madison, Spring Mill Park, and Corydon's state capitol. Great for genealogical researchers, history lovers and antique buffs.

PIONEER COFFEE CAKE

Cake:
1 cup margarine
2 cups sugar
2 eggs
1/2 teaspoon vanilla
1 1/2 cups sour cream

2 cups sifted flour
1 teaspoon baking powder
1/2 teaspoon salt
2 tablespoons cinnamon

Cinnamon Center Mixture:
2 tablespoons melted margarine
1/2 teaspoon vanilla

2 tablespoons flour
4 tablespoons brown sugar

Topping:
3/4 cup chopped nuts
1 teaspoon cinnamon

2 tablespoons brown sugar

Cream Cheese Glaze:
4 oz. softened Philadelphia cream cheese
2 tablespoons melted margarine

1/2 teaspoon vanilla
1 1/2 cups powdered sugar

Cream margarine, sugar and eggs. Fold in vanilla and sour cream. Sift together flour, baking powder and salt. Add to creamed mixture. Sprinkle 2 tablespoons cinnamon throughout batter. Spoon 1/2 cake batter into well-greased tube or bundt pan. Mix all ingredients for Cinnamon Center Mixture so it is crumbly. Dot top of cake batter with this mixture, then sprinkle a little extra cinnamon over it. Pour remainder of batter into pan. Dot over top of batter with rest of Cinnamon Center Mixture, and sprinkle with Topping Mixture. Bake at 350° for 55 - 60 minutes. Let cool a little before removing from pan. Mix Glaze ingredients together to get a loose mixture glaze. Spread over coffee cake while still warm. Cake serves 24, and freezes well.

Submitted by:

The Captains' Quarters
  Bed & Breakfast
R.R. #3, Box 191
Vevay, Indiana 47043
(812) 427-2900
Mr. Leo Hine / Sandy Marsh
$45.00 to $65.00

Continental breakfast
6 rooms
Children allowed
No pets
Restricted smoking

Stately home built in 1838 by riverboat Captain Thomas T. Wright, overlooks Ohio River. Enjoy barges & boats from parlor windows with afternoon tea or lemonade and cookies in evening. Open all year.

POPPY SEED BREAD

3 cups flour
1 1/2 teaspoons salt
1 1/2 teaspoons baking powder
3 eggs
1 1/2 cups oil
2 1/2 cups sugar
1 1/2 cups milk

1 1/2 teaspoons vanilla
1 1/2 teaspoons almond flavoring
1 1/2 teaspoons butter flavoring
1 1/2 tablespoons poppy seeds

Glaze:
1/4 cup orange juice
3/4 cup sugar
1/2 teaspoon vanilla

1/2 teaspoon almond flavoring
1/2 teaspoon butter flavoring

Mix all ingredients together with mixer for 2 minutes or until well blended. Pour into greased bread pans. Bake 1 hour at 350°. After removing from oven, prick top of loaves several times with a fork. Pour glaze over top while still hot. Makes 2 large loaves.

Submitted by:

Varns Guest House
205 South Main St.
P.O. Box 125
Middlebury, Indiana 46540
(219) 825-9666
Carl & Diane Eash
$60.00 to $65.00

Continental plus breakfast
5 rooms, 5 private baths
Children allowed
No pets
No smoking
Mastercard & Visa

Circa 1898. This fourth-generation family home has been lovingly restored to feature turn-of-the-century ambience along with modern luxury. Located in the heart of Amish country, feel free to relax on the porch swing as horse-drawn buggies clip along, or enjoy the warmth of the fireplace during cold weather. Visit many fine restaurants or quaint shops nearby.

PUMPKIN-OATMEAL BARS

1 2/3 cups packed brown sugar
3/4 cup vegetable oil
1 can (16 oz.) pumpkin
4 eggs, slightly beaten
2 cups Bisquick baking mix

1 1/2 cups regular or quick oats
1 tablespoon cinnamon
1/2 teaspoon cloves
1/4 teaspoon nutmeg
1/2 cup chopped pecans

Cream Cheese Frosting:
8 oz. softened cream cheese
1/4 cup softened butter or margarine

1 teaspoon vanilla
2 1/2 cups powdered sugar (more if needed)

Topping:
1/4 cup chopped pecans

Heat oven to 350°. Grease jellyroll pan (15 1/2" x 10 1/2" x 1"). Mix brown sugar, oil, pumpkin and eggs. Stir in baking mix, oats, cinnamon, cloves, nutmeg and pecans. Spread in pan. Bake until wooden pick inserted in center comes out clean, about 30 minutes. Cool. Beat cream cheese, margarine and vanilla until creamy. Stir in powdered sugar until smooth and of spreading consistency. Frost bars. Sprinkle with 1/4 cup pecans for topping. Cut into bars 3" x 1". Refrigerate remaining bars. Makes 50 bars. Freezes well.

Submitted by:

Grandview Guest House
P.O. Box 311, St. Rt. 66
Grandview, Indiana 47615
(812) 649-2817
Gerald & Sandra Bostwick
$38.00 to $45.00

Full breakfast
3 rooms, shared baths

1893 Victorian brick is furnished in period pieces. Lounge area with VCR and cable TV. Homemade cookies & iced tea upon arrival. Breakfast served in family dining room or on brick patio surrounded by roses, daylilies, daffodils and tulips. Near Holiday World, Lincoln State Park, and other attractions.

SIMPLY STRAWBERRY BREAD

3 **cups flour**	4 **eggs - beaten**
2 **cups sugar**	2-**(10 oz.) pkgs.**
1 **teaspoon baking soda**	**Birdseye strawberries**
1 **teaspoon salt**	1 **tub Philadelphia straw-**
1 **cup oil**	**berry cream cheese**

Reserve 1/2 cup strawberries for strawberry cream cheese filling mixture. Mix flour, sugar, soda and salt. Make hole in center, pour in oil, eggs, strawberries (minus 1/2 cup reserved) (process whole ones to chunky purée). Mix with mixer. Pour into 2 greased loaf pans or sheet pan. Bake at 350° for 20-30 minutes. Check after 20 minutes. Blend reserved strawberries with strawberry cream cheese. Use as sandwich spread or frosting.

Submitted by:

Lavendar Lady
130 W. Main Street
Knightstown, Indiana 46148
(317) 345-5400
Judith & Clyde Larrew
$60.00

Full breakfast
3 rooms, 3 private baths
Children, over 10
No pets
No smoking
Mastercard & Visa

Now serving special teas: High Tea and Cream Tea. These are events, not types of tea! English clotted cream is flown in for Cream tea. Tea sandwiches with homemade bread, pastries and sweets are served for High tea.

Lavendar Lady
Bed & Breakfast

circa 1890

SOUR CREAM COFFEE CAKE

1 cup butter	2 cups flour
2 cups sugar	1 teaspoon baking
2 eggs	powder
1 cup sour cream	1/4 teaspoon salt
1 teaspoon vanilla	

Topping:

3/4 cup chopped nuts	4 teaspoons brown sugar
1/2 teaspoon cinnamon	2 teaspoons white sugar

Cream butter and sugar until light and fluffy. Beat in eggs - one at a time. Fold in sour cream and vanilla. Add flour, baking powder and salt. Combine nuts, cinnamon, 4 teaspoons brown sugar and 2 teaspoons white sugar. Mix well. This can be used as a topping, or mixed into the cake in a marble effect. Bake in greased bundt pan at 325° for 1 hour.

Submitted by:

Autumnwood Bed & Breakfast	Continental plus breakfast
165 Autumnwood Lane	9 rooms, 1 private bath
Madison, Indiana 47250	Children allowed
(812) 265-5262	No pets
Jae Breitweiser	Restricted smoking
$55.00 to $82.50	Mastercard & Visa

An 1840 mansion filled with draped canopy beds, marble-topped tables, and handmade bedspreads - all part of our Victorian elegance. Come visit us and have a peaceful weekend getaway.

STRAWBERRY/RHUBARB COFFEE CAKE

Cake:
3 cups flour
1 cup sugar
1 teaspoon baking powder
1 teaspoon salt
1 cup butter, softened
1 cup buttermilk
2 eggs, slightly beaten
1 teaspoon vanilla
Topping:
3/4 cup sugar
1/2 cup flour

Filling:
4 1/2 cups rhubarb, chopped
24 oz. frozen sliced strawberries, thawed
3 tablespoons lemon juice
1 1/2 cups sugar
1/2 cup cornstarch

1/4 cup soft butter

Make filling by combining fruits in saucepan and cooking, covered, over medium heat for 5 minutes, stirring occasionally. Add lemon juice, sugar and cornstarch. Cook, stirring, for 5 minutes or until thickened. Cool.

Make cake by combining flour, sugar, baking powder and salt in large bowl. Cut in butter until mixture is crumbly. Beat together buttermilk, eggs and vanilla; add to flour mixture.

To prepare: Spread 1/2 batter in 3 greased 8" x 8" x 2" baking pans. Spread fruit over batter. Spoon remaining batter in small mounds on top of filling. Mix topping ingredients until crumbly; sprinkle over all. Bake at 375° for 45 minutes. Serve warm. Yields 12 - 16 servings. Freezes well, can be warmed.

Submitted by:

Yount's Mill Inn
3729 Old S.R. 32 West
Crawfordsville, Indiana 47933
(317) 362-5864
Pat & John Hardwick
$35.00 to $50.00

Continental plus breakfast
4 rooms, 2 private baths
Children, over 12
No pets
No smoking
Mastercard & Visa

Built in 1851 as a home and boarding house, both the inn and old mill are in National Register. On Sugar Creek, a pleasant place to walk and relax. Antique shops are plentiful in the area.

TEETOR HOUSE CARAMEL PECAN ROLLS

Dough:
1 envelope active dry yeast
1 cup warm (110°) water, divided
2 teaspoons sugar
1 teaspoon salt
2 cups all-purpose flour

Filling:
3 tablespoons butter, melted
3 tablespoons brown sugar
1/8 teaspoon cinnamon
1/4 cup chopped pecans

Topping:
6 tablespoons light brown sugar
18 pecan halves, broken
6 tablespoons butter, melted
Ground cinnamon

Make dough: Dissolve yeast in 1/4 cup water in large bowl. Stir in remaining 3/4 cup water. Stir in sugar, salt, then flour. Mix well. Cover bowl with cloth & let rest 20 minutes. Turn dough out onto floured board & turn it twice to coat with flour. Pat or roll into 10" x 4" rectangle. Spread top with filling: Brush with melted butter, sprinkle evenly with brown sugar, cinnamon and pecans. Roll up like jelly roll, starting at long side. Cut crosswise with sharp knife into 6 thick slices, about 1 1/2" each. Meanwhile, prepare 6 muffin tins: Place 1 tablespoon each of brown sugar and melted butter, 3 broken pecan halves, and a sprinkle of cinnamon in each. Place slice of dough, cut side down, on top. Place on middle shelf of cold oven. Turn oven to 350° and bake 30 minutes or until golden brown. Serve hot.

Submitted by:

Teetor House
300 West Main Street
Hagerstown, Indiana 47346
(317) 489-4422
Jack & JoAnne Warmoth
$65.00 to $90.00

Full breakfast
4 rooms, 4 private baths
Children allowed
No pets
Restricted smoking
Mastercard & Visa

Elegant 1930's historical mansion on spacious grounds in quaint village. Steinway player piano, chimes, museum and workshop of famous former owner Ralph Teetor. Many unusual amenities.

WOODEN SPOON BREAD

1 loaf frozen white bread
(thawed & softened)
1/2 cup soft butter
(no substitute)
1/4 cup brown sugar
firmly packed

1/4 cup white sugar
1/4 cup flour
1/2 teaspoon vanilla
1 teaspoon cinnamon
1/4 cup walnuts

Shape soft dough into round ball and slightly flatten. Place in greased 9" round pan. Let rise in warm place until doubled. Before baking, with end of wooden spoon or index finger, punch holes in dough. Combine, butter, sugars, flour and vanilla. Fill each hole with mixture. Continue to punch holes and fill until mixture is all used. Spinkle top with cinnamon and nuts. Bake immediately at 350° for 30 minutes or until golden brown and loaf sounds hollow when tapped. Immediately remove from pan and serve warm.

Submitted by:

The Rock House
380 W. Washington Street
Morgantown, Indiana 46160
(812) 597-5100
Donna & George Williams
$50.00 to $70.00

Full breakfast
6 rooms, 2 private baths
Children allowed if supervised
No pets
No smoking

Enjoy a unique home. The home's exterior has dice, geodes, doorknobs, dishes, etc., which were set into the molds for the concrete blocks from which the house was built.

EGG/MEAT DISHES

ARCADIA COUNTRY BREAKFAST

1 lb. bulk sausage
(cooked & drained)
9 large eggs, lightly
beaten
3/4 cup milk, beaten
with eggs

1/4 cup butter, melted
24 oz. hash browned
potatoes
8 oz. shredded Cheddar
cheese

Preheat oven to 350°. Layer sausage on bottom of greased 9" x 13" baking pan. Pour on beaten eggs, milk and butter. Add hash browns on top of egg mixture. Sprinkle cheese over top. Bake at 350° for 1 hour. Serves 9.

Submitted by:

Arcadia House
605 W. Pleasant
Angola, Indiana 46703
(219) 665-2539
Larry & Janelle Rensberger
$45.00 to $65.00

Continental plus breakfast
2 rooms
Children, over 16
No pets
No smoking

Located 2 blocks from campus of Tri-State University. Built in 1909 by Prof. William Bailey, a former fraternity house and mayor's home. Owners' daughter is third generation on Janelle's side to attend Tri-State. Open year-round with comfortable, cozy rooms decorated in antiques.

BAKED EGGS WITH CHEESE

2 large eggs	**3 tablespoons grated**
1 tablespoon	**Cheddar cheese**
heavy cream	**Salt & pepper to taste**

For each individual serving, butter an individual size Welsh rabbit dish. Break the eggs into the dish. Drizzle with heavy cream, salt and pepper. Cover eggs with cheese. Bake in oven at 350° for 15 minutes or until eggs are set.

Submitted by:

Creekwood Inn
Route 20 - 35 at I-94
Michigan City, Indiana 46360
(219) 872-8357
$93.00 to $150.00

Full & Continental breakfast
13 rooms, 13 private baths
Children allowed
No pets
Smoking allowed
Mastercard, Visa, Am Ex

Gracious haven nestled amidst 30 acres of walnut, oak and pine trees, near Willow Creek. Cozy parlor with bay window. Near Indiana Dunes State Park and Warren Dunes State Park in Michigan. Hiking and cross-country skiing in season. Golf, tennis and riding stables nearby.

BREAKFAST BURRITOS

1 lb. pork sausage	4 eggs, beaten
1/4 cup chopped onion	1/2 cup grated Cheddar
1/4 cup chopped red or	cheese
green pepper	Picante sauce
1 1/2 cups frozen hash	Sour cream
browned potatoes	12 - 8" flour tortillas

Brown sausage, add onion & pepper. Cook until tender. Drain. Add potatoes, cook 6 - 8 minutes. Add eggs. Stir. Cook until set. Brown tortillas in hot oil in skillet 5 seconds on each side, or microwave for 45 - 60 seconds. Divide filling among 12 tortillas, sprinkle with cheese. Fold sides, then bottom up. Serve with Picante sauce & sour cream. May be prepared ahead and frozen. Reheat in microwave.

Submitted by:

Windmill Hideaway   Full breakfast
Route #2, Box 48   3 rooms
11380 W. St. Rd. 120   No children
Middlebury, Indiana 46540 No pets
(219) 825-2939   No smoking
Ed & Pat Nelson   Mastercard & Visa
$50.00

Located in a wooded area with a deck. Kick your shoes off and watch squirrels and birds. We try to make our guests feel at home, and help them find points of interest in the area. Near Shipshewana Flea Market - antiques.

BRUNCH QUICHE

1 - 10" pastry for pie crust	1 tablespoon butter or margarine
8 oz. cream cheese, cubed	1 cup cooked ham, bacon or sausage
1 cup milk	1/4 cup pimento
4 eggs, beaten	1/4 teaspoon dill weed or green pepper
1/4 cup chopped onion	

Roll out pastry crust. Bake at 400 ° for 12 - 15 minutes. Combine cream cheese and milk in saucepan. Stir over low heat until smooth. Gradually add cream cheese mixture to eggs, mixing well. Sauté onions in margarine or butter. Add onions and remaining ingredients to cream cheese mixture. Pour into shell. Bake at 350° for 35 - 40 minutes. Serves 8.

Submitted by:

Zimmer Frei Haus B&B
409 N. Main Street
Monticello, Indiana 47960
(219) 583-4061
Kae & John Fuller
$55.00 to $59.00 (Corporate & long term available)

Continental plus breakfast
2 rooms, 2 private baths
Children, under 2
Pets allowed (if kept outside)
Restricted smoking
Mastercard & Visa

1890 Italianate, open year round for distinctive travelers. Minutes from Indiana Beach & Purdue University, 2 hours from Chicago or Indianapolis. Separate television areas, private kitchen available. Breakfast in room, in our breakfast room, or outside, season permitting. Weddings, receptions, business meetings, and afternoon tea upon request.

COUNTRY QUICHE

9" - 10" fresh/frozen deep dish pie crust
6 - 8 slices bacon (crumbled)
1 bunch scallions (chopped)
3 tablespoons olive oil
3 - 4 teaspoons fresh dill (less if using dried dill)
1/2 - 3/4 cup crumbled feta cheese
3 whole eggs
1/2 pint heavy cream
1 - 2 pkgs. spinach or Swiss chard - precook fresh, thaw frozen & squeeze out excess water

Fry bacon, drain, set aside. Sauté scallions in olive oil. Add drained spinach or Swiss chard, crumbled bacon, dill, and crumbled cheese to scallions. Warm through and empty into pie shell. Beat eggs with cream, pour over all ingredients in pie shell. Bake at 350° for one hour or until browned. Can be served warm or is delicious chilled. Makes 8 servings.

Submitted by:

PLAIN and FANCY
Traveler's Accommodations
& Country Store
R.R. #3, Box 62
St. Rd. 135 North
Nashville, Indiana 47448
(812) 988-4537
Suanne Shirley
$60.00 to $65.00

Continental plus breakfast
2 rooms
Children allowed
No pets
Restricted smoking
Mastercard & Visa

Turn of the century log home on 5 acres of deep woods in the most beautiful hill country in Indiana. .8 of a mile (walking distance) from shops and art galleries. Near Brown County State Park, the B.C. Playhouse, & Little Nashville Opry. Secluded, antique furnished, natural environment.

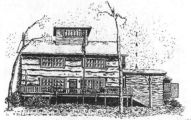

EGG & SAUSAGE CASSEROLE

1 lb. sausage (browned & drained)
6 slices bread (broken up)
2 cups grated Cheddar cheese
2 cups milk

6 eggs, beaten
1 can cream of mushroom soup
1 teaspoon salt
1/4 teaspoon dry mustard

Mix all ingredients well and pour into greased 9" x 13" pan. (Can be mixed the night before, refrigerated; and baked the next morning.) Bake at 325° about 1 hour, until brown and set. Makes 15 servings. Freeze leftovers, can be heated later in microwave.

Submitted by:

Koontz House
  Bed & Breakfast
RR #3, Box 592
Walkerton, Indiana 46574
(219) 586-7090
Les & Jan Davison
$30.00 to $50.00

Continental plus breakfast
4 rooms
Children allowed
No pets
Smoking allowed
Personal checks accepted

Built about 1880 on the west edge of 387 acre Koontz Lake. Large airy bedrooms with color television, swimming area, boat dock. Lakeside restaurant, marina, boat rental, antique shops within walking distance. Potato Creek State Park 12 miles, Plymouth 10 miles, LaPorte 20 miles, South Bend 23 miles.

EGGS FOR A BRUNCH

10 slices bread, crusts
  removed
6 large eggs, beaten
1 pint milk

1/2 teaspoon salt
1 1/2 cups shredded
  cheese
1 stick margarine, melted

Butter a 9" x 13" baking dish. Remove crusts from bread and break into pieces. Put in dish. Mix together eggs, milk and salt. Pour over bread. Sprinkle cheese over top of egg mixture, then drizzle margarine over the top. Refrigerate overnight. Next morning bake at 350° for 45 minutes. Cut into squares and serve. Note: Since the entire house, including kitchen, is provided to guests, and there is no food service, this recipe is from the caterer/housekeeper, Becky Gibbons.

Submitted by:

The Retreat House
8223 W. 550 N.
North Salem, Indiana 46165
(317) 676-6009
John & Marti McCoy
$35.00 each for weekend -
$250 minimum

7 rooms
Children, over 10
No pets
Restricted smoking

Entire 17 room home offered to groups of 8 - 18 people. Antiques, art and collections. Perfect for church groups, card clubs, birdwatchers and nature lovers, family reunions, wedding parties, etc. 3 miles of hiking trails in 100 Acre Wood. Huge treetop deck, heated inground pool, shops nearby.

EGG FRITTATA

2 eggs per serving
Salt & pepper to taste
Vegetable oil
Chopped broccoli
Choppedmushrooms

Chopped green onions
Chopped tomato
Grated cheese of choice
Mild or spicy sausage

Preheat oven to 350°. Beat two eggs per person and season with salt, pepper or whatever seasonings you prefer. Put one drop of vegetable oil in the eggs so that they will not dry out. Sauté sausage. Grease a baking dish with oil and place all the ingredients except eggs into it. You may use as much or little of the listed ingredients as you like. Pour the eggs in last, over the chopped ingredients, sausage and cheese. Do not fill ingredients to top of baking dish as they will rise when baking. Place dish into oven, bake about 40 minutes or until top of eggs are firm. Attempt to leave oven door closed. Eggs cooked in individual baking dishes need only cook 20 minutes. Serve with salsa, fresh muffins, juice, coffee and fruit.

Submitted by:

Le Chateau Delaware
1456 N. Delaware Street
Indianapolis, Indiana 46202
(317) 636-9156
Mignon Wyatt
$75.00 to $85.00 &
10% Indiana state room tax

Full breakfast
5 rooms, 1 private bath
Children, over 10
No pets
Restricted smoking
Mastercard, Visa, Am Ex

This 1906 B&B inn combines the elegance and charm of a turn-of-the-century manor with modern conveniences. We welcome the opportunity to be your hosts for an overnight or extended stay, reception or executive conference. Many Indianapolis activities just minutes away. Warm hospitality.

EGGS SUPREME

6 hard-boiled eggs
8 slices ham

4 English muffins
Grated cheese (topping)

Cream Sauce:
1/4 cup melted butter
3 tablespoons flour
1 - 1 1/2 cups milk

2 tablespoons Dijon
  mustard
Optional: 1/4 of a green
  pepper, chopped fine

Peel hard-boiled eggs and chop fine. Make cream sauce by adding flour to melted butter. Mix well, add milk to thickness you like, and add mustard. Add chopped eggs to cream sauce. Add green pepper if desired. Place slice of ham on English muffin. Top with egg mixture and sprinkle with grated cheese. Place on cookie sheet in 375° oven until cheese melts. Serves 8.

Submitted by:

Queen Anne Inn
420 W. Washington
South Bend, Indiana 46601
(219) 234-5959
Pauline & Bob Medhurst
$65.00 to $89.00

Full breakfast
5 rooms, 5 private baths
Children allowed
No pets
Restricted smoking
Mastercard, Visa, Am Ex

1893 Victorian noted for its leaded glass windows and Frank Lloyd Wright-designed bookcases. Furnished in antiques. Victorian getaway special includes dinner, a museum tour and carriage ride. Near downtown South Bend and Notre Dame.

HAM STRATA

6 slices white bread	1/2 teaspoon salt
6 slices Cheddar cheese	1/2 teaspoon prepared
4 eggs	mustard
2 cups milk	1 teaspoon minced
	onion
Topping:	
Ground ham	**Crumbled bacon**

Trim crusts from bread, lay in pan. Lay cheese slices over bread. Mix remaining ingredients and pour over bread and cheese. Let set overnight in refrigerator. Next day sprinkle ground ham or crumbled bacon on top. Bake at 350° for 30 minutes. Serves 6.

Submitted by:

Friendliness with a Flair
5214 E. 20th Pl.
Indianapolis, Indiana 46218
(317) 356-3149
Loretta Whitten
$45.00

Full breakfast
2 rooms, 2 private baths
Children, over 10
No pets
Restricted smoking
Cash or personal check

Tastefully furnished clean rooms. Outside dining in Florida Room, season permitting. Dining in family room or dining room otherwise. Varied menus and table settings.

MA'S SCRAMBLED EGGS

6 eggs
1 tablespoon Bacos
(imitation bacon bits)
1/2 cup milk
1/2 teaspoon prepared
mustard

1/4 teaspoon hickory
smoked salt
1/4 teaspoon salt
1/4 teaspoon black
pepper
1 cup grated mild
Cheddar cheese

Spray Pam in 3-quart sauce pan. Beat eggs well, add and mix well the next 6 ingredients. Pour into sauce pan. Add cheese. Cook on medium heat and stir occasionally to keep from sticking. Serves 4.

Submitted by:

Folke Family Farm Inn
18595 Pribble Road
Lawrenceburg, Indiana 47025
(812) 537-4486
JoAnn Folke
$40.00 to $60.00

Full breakfast
4 rooms, 2 private baths
Children allowed
No pets
Restricted smoking
Mastercard & Visa

Historic Hoosier homestead farm in scenic Southeastern Indiana, approximately 30 minutes from downtown Cincinnati, Ohio. Quiet, relaxed atmosphere where guests can stroll walking trails and experience panoramic views. Share nature with abundant birds, rabbits and deer.

MEAT POTATO QUICHE

3 tablespoons vegetable oil	1 lb. browned sausage, drained
3 cups coarsely shredded raw potatoes	2 tablespoons chopped green pepper
1 1/2 cups grated Cheddar cheese	1 1/2 cups milk
1/4 cup chopped onion	5 eggs
	Parsley

Place potatoes in oil in 9" x 13" x 2" pan and bake potatoes for 15 minutes at 400°. Brown and drain sausage. Layer cheese, onion, sausage and green pepper over potatoes. Beat milk and eggs; pour over other ingredients. Sprinkle with parsley. Return to oven, bake 30 minutes. Serves 12 - 15. Recipe provided by Mallory Miniear, caterer for White Hill Manor.

Submitted by:

White Hill Manor	Full breakfast
2513 East Center Street	8 rooms, 8 private baths
Warsaw, Indiana 46580	Children allowed
(219) 269-6933	No pets
Gladys Deloe, Mgr.	Restricted smoking
$75.00 to $112.00 (doubles)	Mastercard, Visa, Am Ex

Elegant, restored English Tudor mansion in heart of Lake Country. Great water recreation, next door to Wagon Wheel Theatre and restaurant. Great antiques in nearby Pierceton and Silver Lake. An hour from Amish country.

MELODIE'S BREAKFAST TREAT

**1 lb. sausage or diced
ham
1 cup sharp shredded
cheese**

**4 slices bread, broken
into pieces
6 eggs
2 cups milk**

Fry meat and drain. Layer meat in bottom of pan, put cheese on next layer. Put half of bread pieces on next layer. Beat eggs, add milk. Pour over casserole. Put remaining bread pieces on top of casserole dish. Refrigerate until morning and bake at 350° for 45 minutes.

Submitted by:

Country Bed & Breakfast
27727 CR 36
Goshen, Indiana 46526
(219) 862-2748
Vernon & Bertha Miller
$30.00 to $35.00

Continental plus breakfast
2 rooms, 1 private bath
Children allowed
No pets
No smoking

Enjoy our country hospitality surrounded by fields of growing grain, enjoy lovely walks to our woods. Air-conditioned guest rooms, home built for handicapped. Relax and visit with us.

NESTED EGGS

Canadian bacon, bacon
  or ham

8 eggs, separated
4 English muffins

Sauce:
4 egg yolks
3 tablespoons fresh
  lemon juice

1 cup unsalted butter
Cayenne pepper

Preheat oven to 375°. If using bacon, precook and set aside. If using ham, lightly cook to remove water. Butter and lightly toast muffin halves. Separate egg yolks from whites, being careful not to break yolks. Whip whites to a stiff consistency. Top half of a muffin (crust down) with meat, then with whipped egg white. Hollow out center with spoon. These can be particularly attractive if you pipe the egg white. Roll the egg yolk back into center of the muffin. Bake in oven until yolks are just set on the top (10 - 15 minutes). Prepare sauce while eggs are baking. For sauce: In double boiler place egg yolks and juice and 1/4 cup butter in pan over simmering water. Stir with wire whip until butter is melted. Continue adding butter in small portions until all is used. Season to taste with pepper. Top lightly browned eggs with sauce and serve.

Submitted by:

Beiger Mansion Inn
317 Lincoln Way East
Mishawaka, Indiana 46544
(219) 256-0365 or
1-800-437-0131
Ron Montandon and
  Phil Robinson
$60.00 to $85.00

5 rooms, 5 private baths
Children allowed, but no play
  areas
No pets
No smoking
Mastercard, Visa, Am Ex, Carte
Blanche, Discover, Diners
Club

Neo-classical limestone mansion built in 1907. Palatial rooms, once a gathering place for local society, now graciously welcome guests. Notre Dame, St. Mary's and Indiana University in South Bend are minutes away. On National Registry of Historic Places.

NORMANDIE'S "ALMOST EGGS BENEDICT"

1/2 toasted & buttered English muffin
1 piece cooked Canadian bacon
1 piece thinly sliced Swiss cheese

1 poached egg

Garnishes:
Parsley sprig, pimento piece, canned Mandarin orange slice

Take 1/2 toasted and buttered English muffin, place one piece of cooked Canadian bacon on it, then a piece of Swiss cheese cut into a circle with hamburger patty maker. Top with poached egg, garnished with your choice of garnishes listed. Quick and easy. Serves any number easily. Can toast large quantities in oven. Recipe makes 1 individual serving. Note: Our guests select groceries from a menu. We stock kitchen. They cook; we clean up.

Submitted by:

Mindheims' Inn
R.R. #5, Box 592
Nashville, Indiana 47448
(812) 988-2590
Art & Normandie Mindheim
$50.00 to $65.00 (Oct.), plus
5% state sales tax & 5% inn tax

Full breakfast (guests cook)
Complete apartment -
air-conditioned
Private bath
Children allowed
Pets allowed
Smoking restricted to deck

Enjoy the view of the woods, stream and birds from your deck or stay in your own cozy country apartment and read, play games, try the organ or watch television. Visit nearby attractions of Nashville and Brown County: the shops, parks, Little Nashville Opry or Ski World.

"OLD HOOSIER HOUSE" BAKED EGGS

12 hard-cooked eggs
(deviled with salt and
pepper and mayonnaise
only)

Topping:
6 slices crisply fried
bacon, crumbled

Sauce:
6 tablespoons butter
6 tablespoons flour
2 cups milk
1 lb. Velveeta cheese
(cubed)

1 1/2 cups bread crumbs
sautéed in butter (opt.)

Place deviled eggs in 9" x 12" glass baking dish. To make sauce: Melt butter, add flour and milk, and stir over heat until thick. Add cubed cheese and stir until melted. Pour sauce over eggs and top with crumbled bacon. Bake at 325° for 1/2 hour. Makes 6 - 8 servings. (Optional: Add bread crumbs over the top.)

Submitted by:

Old Hoosier House
Route 2, Box 299-1
Knightstown, Indiana 46148
(317) 345-2969
Jean & Tom Lewis
$38.00 to $63.00

Full breakfast
4 rooms, 3 private baths
Children allowed
No pets
Restricted smoking

Enjoy true Indiana country living, with a sunny patio and view of an 18-hole golf course, or dining in the intimate breakfast room. Library and sitting room with sofa, chairs and television, also a deck and front porch. Hiking, bicycling, bird watching and sightseeing are popular pastimes. Central air conditioning.

QUICHE

1 frozen unbaked pie
  crust
4 eggs
1 can cream of
  mushroom soup
1/2 cup cream

1 cup shredded Cheddar
  cheese
6 slices bacon, crisp
  and crumbled
1/2 cup cooked chopped
  broccoli
Nutmeg

Mix together eggs, soup, cream, cheese, bacon and broccoli. Pour into pie shell, sprinkle nutmeg on top. Bake at 350° for 50 minutes. Cool 10 minutes. Serve.

Submitted by:

Fruitt Basket Inn
116 W. Main St.
North Manchester, IN 46962
(219) 982-2443
Sharon & Randy Fruitt
$45.00

Full breakfast
3 rooms
Children allowed
No pets
No smoking

Built at the turn of the century and for many years served as a Tourist Home and Boarding House. Inn preserves the past and complements the owners' interior decorating business. Reservations are required.

ROSEWOOD MANSION'S QUICHE

1/2 lb. cooked bacon
4 oz. can mushrooms
Pinch of basil
Pinch of dried mustard
1/2 lb. Monterey Jack cheese

1/3 lb. Baby Swiss cheese
5 eggs
1/2 cup milk
1 - 9" deep dish pie shell

In the unbaked pie shell, layer cooked bacon, then mushrooms. Sprinkle basil and mustard, add Monterey Jack cheese and Swiss cheese. Then mix eggs with milk and pour over quiche. Bake at 400° for 15 minutes, then at 350° for 45 minutes. Serves 6.

Submitted by:

Rosewood Mansion Inn
54 N. Hood
Peru, Indiana 46970
(317) 472-7151
Fax # (317) 472-5575
Carman & Zoyla Henderson
$55.00 to $115.00

Full breakfast
9 rooms, 9 private baths
Children, over 12
Pets allowed
Restricted smoking
Mastercard, Visa, Am Ex,
  Discover, Diners' Club

1878 mansion, 3 blocks from center of town, on one acre setting with wrought iron fence. 3-story open staircase of tiger oak, beautiful woodwork and stained glass. All guest rooms have telephones and color/remote televisions. Near tennis, golf, swimming, historical tours and four museums.

SAUSAGE AND EGG CASSEROLE

1 lb. bulk sausage, browned and drained
6 eggs, beaten
2 cups milk
1 teaspoon salt
Pepper
1 teaspoon dry mustard
1 1/2 teaspoon Worcestershire sauce
6 - 8 slices bread (cubed without crust)
1 cup shredded Cheddar or Swiss cheese

Mix all ingredients together and pour into a 9" x 13" pan. Refrigerate overnight. Bake at 325° for 45 minutes or until browned and firm. Makes 10 - 12 servings.

Submitted by:

Garber's Guesthouse
24641 C.R. 142
Goshen, Indiana 46526
(219) 831-3740
Marion & Phyllis Garber
$40.00 to $45.00

Full breakfast
3 rooms, 1 private bath
Children allowed
No pets
No smoking

Cape Cod style, newly built home set back a distance from the road on a large, wooded lot. Quiet, country setting with a large deck and sunroom. Close to Amish settlements and only 30 miles from Notre Dame.

SAUSAGE QUICHE

1 - 9" pie shell	1 small finely chopped
1/2 lb. country style	onion
sausage	2 eggs
1 cup grated Cheddar	1 - 12 oz. can evapor-
cheese	ated milk
1 tablespoon flour	Parsley

Brown sausage, drain. Place in unbaked pie shell. Sprinkle grated cheese, flour and onion on top. Beat eggs and milk, pour over mixture in pie shell. Sprinkle parsley on top. Bake at 350 ° for 45 minutes or until set.

Submitted by:

White Birch Bed & Breakfast
17200 Institutional Drive
Goshen, Indiana 46526
(219) 533-3763
Karen Fergison
$55.00 to $65.00

Continental plus breakfast
2 rooms, 2 private baths
Children allowed
No pets
No smoking
Mastercard & Visa

Relax on this 3 acre certified wildlife habitat, many species of birds and butterflies. Guests enjoy their own spacious living and dining rooms, or the frontier room with massive split stone fireplace. Located between Shipshewana and Nappanee. Come discover that hospitality is not just a word . . . but a way of life.

SMOKED CHEDDAR QUICHE

1 uncooked deep dish
  pie crust
2 tablespoons Dijon
  mustard
1/2 cup shredded
  smoked Cheddar
  cheese

1 small bunch fresh
  spinach leaves, cut in
  1/2" strips
2 cups fresh sliced
  mushrooms
8 oz. pkg. EggBeaters
1 cup milk

Preheat oven to 400°. Brush mustard on bottom of pie crust. Steam/sauté mushrooms on low heat in 1 tablespoon of water and cover till soft. Add spinach leaves and cook till wilted. Drain liquid. Meanwhile, sprinkle cheese in pie crust. Add cooked mushrooms and spinach. Mix EggBeaters and milk in separate bowl, then add to pie crust. Cook for 15 minutes at 400°, then for 30 minutes at 325°.

Submitted by:

Home of the Royal Stones
P.O. Box 30251
Indianapolis, Indiana 46230
(317) 254-8005 (home)
Joan Schneider
$65.00 to $70.00

Full breakfast
1 room, 1 private bath
No children
No pets
No smoking

Beautifully furnished contemporary master bedroom suite with deck. Enjoy delightful summer gardens, privacy and quiet surroundings, and toasty wintertime fires. Collection of stones from around the world. Delicious and unusual breakfasts served.

SPINACH QUICHE

1 - 12 oz. pkg. Stouffer's spinach soufflé
1 deep dish pie crust
3/4 lb. sausage
2 teaspoons chopped onion
1/2 cup chopped mushrooms

2 tablespoons butter, melted
2 eggs, beaten
3 tablespoons milk
3/4 cup cheese

Prepare spinach soufflé according to directions on package. Prick pie crust all over and bake at 400° for 7 - 10 minutes. Brown sausage and pour off fat. Sauté onion and mushrooms in butter. Combine with beaten eggs and milk. Mix with the soufflé and pour into the crust. Arrange cheese and sausage decoratively on top. Bake at 400° for 25 - 30 minutes. Let stand 5 minutes before slicing. Makes 6 servings. Note: Use pork sausage with Cheddar cheese. Use Italian sausage with mozzarella cheese.

Submitted by:

Candlewyck Inn
331 W. Washington Blvd.
Fort Wayne, Indiana 46802
(219) 424-2643
Jan & Bob Goehringer
$45.00 to $60.00

Full breakfast, weekends
Continental plus breakfast, weekdays
5 rooms
No children
No pets
Restricted smoking
Mastercard, Visa, Am Ex

Built in 1914, California Craftsman style bungalow, furnished with antiques and brass. Wood floors, handsome wallcoverings and accessories. Lovely beveled and stained glass windows throughout. Oak beamed ceilings in the parlor and dining room add to this charming home.

WAKE UP CASSEROLE

2 cups seasoned croutons
1 cup shredded Cheddar cheese
1 - 4 oz. can mushroom pieces, drained
1 1/2 lbs. country-fresh sausage, browned & crumbled
1/2 cup chopped onion

6 eggs
2 cups milk
1/2 teaspoon salt
1/2 teaspoon pepper
1/2 teaspoon dry mustard
1 - 10 3/4 oz. can cream of mushroom soup
1/2 cup milk

Place croutons in greased 9" x 13" x 2" pan. Top with cheese and mushrooms. Brown sausage and onion; drain and spread over cheese. Beat eggs with 2 cups of milk and seasonings; pour over sausage. Cover and refrigerate overnight. (May be frozen at this point). Mix soup with 1/2 cup milk and spread on top. Bake at 325° for 1 hour. Serves 8.

Submitted by:

The Thorpe House
Clayborne Street
P.O. Box 36
Metamora, Indiana 47030
(317) 647-5425 or 932-2365
Mike & Jean Owens
$60.00 to $100.00

Full breakfast
5 rooms, 3 private baths
Children allowed
Pets allowed, by prior arrangement
Smoking allowed
Mastercard & Visa

1840 Canal town home, where steam engine still brings passenger cars, and gristmill still grinds cornmeal. Antiques and country accessories, family-style public dining room, country breakfast. Over 100 shoppes in quaint village. Open April through Christmas.

MISCELLANEOUS

Beverages, Cereal & Fruit Dishes

ALMOST-A-MEAL BREAKFAST DRINK

2 - 5 1/4 oz. cans
  pineapple tidbits
2 medium bananas
1/2 cup milk

16 ozs. pineapple
  sherbet or lowfat yogurt
2 - 4 tablespoons
  orange juice

In food processor combine all ingredients. Blend until smooth. Makes 4 servings. Recipe may be doubled for more servings.

Submitted by:

Maple Leaf Inn
  Bed & Breakfast
831 N. Grand
Connersville, Indiana 47331
(317) 825-7099
Gary & Karen Lanning
$45.00 to $55.00

Continental plus breakfast
4 rooms, 4 private baths
Children allowed
No pets
Restricted smoking
Mastercard & Visa

Surrounded by lovely maple trees, this 1860's Victorian home offers warm hospitality. Bedrooms furnished with period furniture and paintings by local artists. Area attractions include state parks, antique shops, Indiana's largest lake and Whitewater Valley Railroad and Old Metamora.

APPLE SALAD

6 - 8 unpeeled diced red apples	Dressing:
	2 eggs
1 can drained pineapple tidbits	Pineapple juice
	3/4 cup sugar
1 cup seedless red grapes (halved)	2 tablespoons flour
	2 tablespoons butter
2 diced bananas	
1 cup mini-marshmallows	1 cup whipping cream or
Nuts (optional)	Cool Whip

Mix fruit, marshmallows and nuts together. Beat eggs, add juice, sugar, and flour, and cook until thickened, then add butter. Cool. Pour cooled dressing over apple mixture. When ready to serve, add whipped cream and mix all together lightly. Makes 12 - 15 servings.

Submitted by:

Bontreger Guest Rooms
10766 C. R. 16
Middlebury, Indiana 46540
(219) 825-2647
Tom & Ruby Bontreger
$30.00 to $35.00

Continental breakfast
2 rooms, 2 private baths
Children allowed
No pets
No smoking

Pleasant country atmosphere in this newly remodeled home, located between Middlebury & Shipshewana in the heart of an Amish neighborhood. Easy access to area restaurants, gift shops & Flea Market. Breakfast served in sun room overlooking the swimming pool.

BLUEBERRY SALAD

1 (6 oz.) pkg. raspberry gelatin
2 cups boiling water
1 1/2 cups cold water and ice

1 cup crushed pine-apple, undrained
2 cups blueberries, drained (or pie filling)

Topping:
8 oz. cream cheese, softened
1/2 cup sugar

1 cup sour cream or Cool Whip
1 teaspoon vanilla
1/2 cup chopped pecans

Stir gelatin and boiling water together until dissolved. Add cold water and ice, stirring to cool. Stir in pineapple and blueberries. Pour into 9" x 13" dish. Chill until set. Beat all topping ingredients except pecans together until smooth. Spread over salad. Sprinkle pecans over the top.

Submitted by:

Patchwork Quilt Country Inn
11748 County Road 2
Middlebury, Indiana 46540
(219) 825-2417
Maxine Zook & Susan Thomas
$50.95 to $95.00

Full breakfast
9 rooms, 6 private baths
Children, over 5
No pets
No smoking
Mastercard & Visa

Patchwork Quilt Country Inn is a centennial farm, tucked away in northern Indiana country. Patchwork Quilt offers fine dining and is rated one of top 10 restaurants in Indiana, with overnight lodging and tours which will take you to meet our Amish friends.

BREAKFAST FRUIT CUP

2 - 16 oz. cans apricots, chopped	5 bananas, diced
1 - 16 oz. can pineapple	2 cups water
1 - 12 oz. can frozen orange concentrate	1 cup sugar
	2 tablespoons lemon juice

Mix well and freeze in small cups or a large pan. You may also use fresh peaches, white or red grapes, or maraschino cherries.

Submitted by:

Bessinger's Hillfarm Wildlife
Refuge Bed & Breakfast
4588 S. R. 110
Tippecanoe, Indiana 46570
(219) 223-3288
$45.00

Full breakfast
2 rooms, 2 private baths
Children, over 10
No pets
Restricted smoking

This cozy log home overlooking water area with 33 islands, has 2 guest rooms, plus a loft with a hide-a-bed. Hiking, canoeing, cross country skiing, and fishing are available.

BREAKFAST SHAKE

1 cup plain yogurt
1/2 cup milk
1 cup fruit (whatever is
  in season)
1 banana

4 teaspoons honey
1 teaspoon vanilla
1 tablespoon peanut
butter

Combine all ingredients in blender, blend until smooth. Makes four - 1 cup servings.

Submitted by:

Waterford Bed & Breakfast
3004 South Main St.
Goshen, Indiana 46526
(219) 533-6044
Judith Forbes
$45.00

Full breakfast
3 rooms, 2 private baths
Children, over 8
No pets
Restricted smoking

Located in heart of Amish country, surrounded by two acres of landscaped trees and gardens. Rooms tastefully and completely furnished with antiques gathered from Indiana area. Near Amish Acres Art Festival, Shipshewana Flea Market, and Mennonite Relief Sale in Goshen.

FRUIT SOUP

12 oz. prunes	1 tablespoon lemon juice
7 oz. dried peaches	1 tablespoon lemon rind
6 oz. dried apricots	(grated)
3 oz. dried apple chunks	2 tablespoons minute
8 oz. light raisins	tapioca
2 oz. currants	1/2 - 1 cup sugar
2 quarts water	1 cinnamon stick
(more or less)	1 can red cherries
1/4 cup orange juice	2 pears, peeled, cored &
1 tablespoon orange rind	sliced
(grated)	

Put dried fruit in 4-quart microwave-safe casserole with 1 1/2 quarts water. Microwave on 50% power for 10 minutes. Stir, allow to stand 30 minutes. Add orange juice & rind, lemon juice & rind, tapioca, sugar and cinnamon stick. Cook on High power for 10 minutes. Stir. Continue cooking at 10 - 50% power, stirring at 10 minute intervals until fruit is almost tender. Add water as needed. Add cherries (and juice) and sliced pears, and cook another 10 minutes. This recipe can be adjusted so thickness is what you prefer, and you can use whatever kinds of fruit you like. It keeps several weeks in refrigerator. Can be served warm or cold. Makes 3 - 4 quarts of soup.

Submitted by:

Davis House	Continental plus breakfast
1010 W. Wabash Ave.	4 rooms, 4 private baths
Crawfordsville, Indiana 47933	Children allowed
(317) 364-0461	Pets allowed, with prior notice
Jan Stearns	Restricted smoking
$35.00 to $60.00	Mastercard, Visa, Am Ex,
	Discover

1870's Italianate mansion in historic Crawfordsville. Country furnishings in spacious rooms. Near Wabash College, Old Jail Museum, Lane Place and Lew Wallace Study, as well as antique, boutique and specialty shops.

GRANOLA

10 cups oatmeal
1 cup coconut
3/4 cup sunflower seeds
1 cup nuts (pecans, al-
  monds, peanuts - raw)
8 rounded tablespoons
  Shaklee Fiber Blend
  daily mix (opt.)

1 1/3 cups brown sugar
3/4 cup water
1 1/3 cups vegetable oil
1 tablespoon vanilla
1 tablespoon maple
  flavoring
2 teaspoons salt

Mix together all ingredients. Toast in 325° oven, stirring every 10 minutes, 4 or 5 times. Variation: Adding 1 cup applesauce or 3/4 cup more water makes it more chunky. Makes 20 - 25 servings.

Submitted by:

Country Lane Guest House
14737 S.R. 4
Goshen, Indiana 46526
(219) 533-1631
Harley & Betty Troyer
$35.00 to $65.00

Continental plus breakfast
4 rooms, 2 private baths
Children, over 10
No pets
Restricted smoking
Mastercard & Visa

Contemporary house in middle of Amish country. White tail deer and geese can be observed from deck overlooking farm pond. Near Shipshewana Flea Market and Amish Acres in Nappanee. Rooms are air-conditioned and decorated with a touch of country.

HOT FRUIT COMPOTE

1 - 20 oz. can pineapple chunks
1 - 16 oz. can peach slices
1 - 16 oz. can pear halves
1 - 16 oz. can apricot halves
1 jar maraschino cherries

Orange Sauce:
1/3 cup sugar
2 tablespoons cornstarch
1/4 teaspoon salt
1/2 cup light corn syrup
1 cup orange juice
2 tablespoons orange rind

Drain fruit, arrange in a 9" x 13" baking dish with cherries in hollows. Set aside. Combine Orange Sauce ingredients in pan, heat to a boil. Remove, pour sauce over fruit compote. Bake at 350° for 30 minutes. Makes 12 servings.

Submitted by:

Hill Top Country Inn
1733 C. R. 28
Auburn, Indiana 46706
(219) 281-2298
Chuck & Becky Derrow
$35.00 to $50.00

Full breakfast
3 bed chambers,
  1 private bath
Children allowed
No pets
No smoking

Historic farm home, former tourist farmhouse from 1925 to 1940's. Bed chambers and sitting rooms are decorated with quilts, antiques and stenciling. Auburn Cord Duesenburg Museum, Pokagon State Park, and many lakes are some area attractions.

MARINATED FRUIT

3 cups honeydew melon and/or cantaloupeballs

1 - 13 1/2 oz. can pineapple chunks, drained

1 - 11 oz. can mandarin oranges, drained

1 cup strawberries, cleaned & hulled

1 - 6 oz. can frozen grapefruit juice or frozen lemonade

1/4 cup orange marmalade

Combine all fruits in a bowl. Combine grapefruit juice or lemonade and marmalade. Pour over fruits, stir gently. Chill at least 2 hours before serving. Yield: 6 cups.

Submitted by:

Home Bed & Breakfast
21166 Clover Hill Court
South Bend, Indiana 46614
(219) 291-0535
Mark & Joyce Funderburg
$35.00 to $45.00

Advanced registration only
Full breakfast
3 rooms, shared baths
Children allowed
No pets
No smoking

Warm, homelike environment awaits you in European traditional B&B. Located in a quiet residential court, overlooking a pond, guest rooms are our "empty nest" rooms. Minutes from Notre Dame, downtown and Potato Creek State Park. Amish communities and Lake Michigan beaches an hour away.

"MAY DAY" FRUIT BASKETS

2 large Shredded Wheat
biscuits
1/4 cup coconut
1 tablespoon brown
sugar

1/4 cup margarine,
melted
Approximately 3 cups
fresh fruit
Ground nutmeg or
cinnamon

Crumble Shredded Wheat biscuits; stir in coconut and sugar. Drizzle with melted margarine, toss to coat. Line six - 6 oz. custard cups or muffin cups with foil. Press mixture onto bottoms and up sides of lined cups. Bake at 350° for 10 minutes or until crisp. Cool in cups. Remove from cups by lifting foil. Peel foil off baskets. Fill cups with fresh fruit (approximately 1/2 cup fruit per basket) and sprinkle with nutmeg or cinnamon. Makes 6 baskets.

Submitted by:

Wraylyn Knoll
Greasy Creek Road
P.O. Box 481
Nashville, Indiana 47448
(812) 988-0733
Marcia & Larry Wray
$50.00 to $80.00

Full breakfast (weekends)
Continental breakfast
 (weekdays)
5 rooms, 5 private baths
Children allowed
No pets
Restricted smoking
Mastercard & Visa

Outstanding view from hilltop on 12 acres, fishing pond, outdoor pool, running creek at bottom of hill. Only 1 mile from bustling village of Nashville in heart of Brown County.

PAN-FRIED BREAD

3 lbs. flour	1 tablespoon butter
1 level tablespoon salt	2 tablespoons sugar
4 tablespoons Crisco	1 1/2 cups warm water
1 pkg. yeast	2 tablespoons Wesson
1 cup warm water	oil

Mix flour, salt and Cisco in large bowl. In small bowl mix yeast, 1 cup warm water, butter and sugar. Wait for 10 minutes or foam. Add yeast mixture and about 1 1/2 cups of warm water to flour mixture in large bowl. Work for 5 minutes. Add Wesson oil to take stickiness out. Cover and let rise for 1 1/2 to 2 hours. Then knead second time for 5 minutes. Tear off small bits (roll size), put in hot frying pan with a little Wesson oil. Top with powdered sugar, jam, syrup or fruit, or whatever you like! Makes 30 pieces.

Submitted by:

Lomax Station
RR #1, Box 128
San Pierre, IN 46374
(219) 896-5353
Michael & Rosie Anthony
$35.00 to $50.00

Full breakfast
3 rooms, 3 private baths
Children allowed
Pets allowed
Smoking allowed

Established in 1853 on the south bank of the Kankakee River, a former railroad and pipeline town. Now a restored home for our bed & breakfast and fine family dining. Friday nights we fly fresh fish into our own air field. All you can eat Sunday buffet. Home-baked breads and rolls. Open only Friday nights and Sunday mornings to the public.

SUNSHINE RISER

1 - 6 oz. can orange
   juice concentrate
1 cup water

4 ice cubes
1 cup vanilla ice cream

Blend ingredients in an electric blender. Add more water if too thick. Serve in long-stemmed wineglasses. Variation: You may substitute cranberry or pineapple/banana concentrates if you wish. Makes 3 servings.

Submitted by:

Allison House Inn
P.O. Box 546
90 S. Jefferson
Nashville, Indiana 47448
(812) 988-0814
Bob & Tammy Galm
$85.00

Continental plus breakfast
5 rooms, 5 private baths
Children, over 12
No pets
No smoking

In the heart of the village within the center of Brown County's arts and crafts colony. 1883 restored Victorian emphasizes charm, coziness and comfort.

VEGETABLE BAR

2 pkgs. crescent rolls
8 oz. cream cheese
1/2 cup sour cream
1/2 cup Kraft
 mayonnaise
1 envelope Hidden
 Valley Ranch dressing
1 cup cauliflower (finely
 chopped)

1 cup broccoli (finely
 chopped)
3/4 cup canned
 mushrooms
1/2 cup tomatoes (opt.)
1/2 cup green peppers
 (finely chopped)
1/2 cup ham bits
1 cup grated cheese

Spread rolls out and press on a pizza pan sheet. Bake at 375° for 8 minutes, and let cool. Mix together cream cheese, sour cream, mayonnaise, and Hidden Valley Ranch dressing with a beater. Spread over crescent rolls. Then add vegetables in layers. Put ham bits on top of vegetables. Top with grated cheese. Makes 12 servings.

Submitted by:

Mary's Place
305 Eugene Drive
Middlebury, Indiana 46540
(219) 825-2429
$40.00 to $45.00

Continental breakfast
2 rooms
Children allowed
No pets
No smoking

Private entrance with two bedrooms. Air-conditioned. Private family room with cable television.

INDEX OF INNS

ORDER FORMS

The INDIANA BED & BREAKFAST ASSOCIATION COOKBOOK and DIRECTORY

I would like to order *The* INDIANA BED & BREAKFAST ASSOCIATION COOKBOOK and DIRECTORY. I have indicated the quantity below. <u>MAIL ORDER TO</u>: Winters Publishing, P.O. Box 501, Greensburg, IN 47240.

_____ Indiana B & B Cookbook and Directory $9.95 each _____

Shipping Charge $2.00 each _____

Sales Tax (Indiana residents <u>ONLY</u>) $ .60 each _____

TOTAL _____

Please send to:

Name: _____

Address: _____

City: _____   State: _____   Zip: _____

BREAKFAST COOKBOOK: FAVORITE RECIPES FROM AMERICA'S BED & BREAKFAST INNS

This book, also by Tracy & Phyllis Winters, is 320 pages long and contains recipes from over 300 Bed & Breakfast Inns throughout America. <u>MAIL ORDER TO</u>: Winters Publishing, P.O. Box 501, Greensburg, IN 47240.

_____ BREAKFAST COOKBOOK $10.95 each _____

Shipping Charge $2.00 each _____

Sales Tax (Indiana residents <u>ONLY</u>) $ .65 each _____

TOTAL _____

Please send to:

Name: _____

Address: _____

City: _____   State: _____   Zip: _____

ORDER FORMS

The INDIANA BED & BREAKFAST ASSOCIATION COOKBOOK and DIRECTORY

I would like to order *The* INDIANA BED & BREAKFAST ASSOCIATION COOKBOOK and DIRECTORY. I have indicated the quantity below. <u>MAIL ORDER TO</u>: Winters Publishing, P.O. Box 501, Greensburg, IN 47240.

_____ Indiana B & B Cookbook and Directory $9.95 each _____

Shipping Charge $2.00 each _____

Sales Tax (Indiana residents <u>ONLY</u>) $ .60 each _____

TOTAL _____

Please send to:

Name:

Address:

City: State: Zip:

BREAKFAST COOKBOOK: FAVORITE RECIPES FROM AMERICA'S BED & BREAKFAST INNS

This book, also by Tracy & Phyllis Winters, is 320 pages long and contains recipes from over 300 Bed & Breakfast Inns throughout America. <u>MAIL ORDER TO</u>: Winters Publishing, P.O. Box 501, Greensburg, IN 47240.

_____ BREAKFAST COOKBOOK $10.95 each _____

Shipping Charge $2.00 each _____

Sales Tax (Indiana residents <u>ONLY</u>) $ .65 each _____

TOTAL _____

Please send to:

Name:

Address:

City: State: Zip:

NOTES

NOTES

NOTES

NOTES

NOTES